THE LIBRARY OF
AMERICAN
LIVES AND TIMES™

# HAYM SALOMON

## Patriot Banker of the American Revolution

Jane Frances Amler

BPMS MEDIA CENTER

The Rosen Publishing Group's
PowerPlus Books™
New York

*Dedicated to Larry, Scott, and Michael*

Published in 2004 by The Rosen Publishing Group, Inc.
29 East 21st Street, New York, NY 10010

First Edition

*Editor's Note: All quotations have been reproduced as they appeared in the letters and diaries from which they were borrowed. No correction was made to the inconsistent spelling that was common in that time period.*

**Library of Congress Cataloging-in-Publication Data**

Amler, Jane Frances.
Haym Salomon : patriot banker of the American Revolution / Jane Frances Amler.— 1st ed.
    v. cm.— (The library of American lives and times)
Includes bibliographical references and index.
Contents: The early years—The Revolution begins—The battle for the North Country—A Rebel with a cause—Marriage, family, and a narrow escape—Philadelphia, the heart of the rebellion—Salomon comes to the aid of Morris and Washington—Salomon serves a new nation—America, the first years of the Republic—Salomon's fight for religious freedom.
  ISBN 0-8239-6629-1 (lib. bdg.)
1. Salomon, Haym, 1740–1785—Juvenile literature. 2. United States—History—Revolution, 1775–1783—Biography—Juvenile literature.
3. United States—History—Revolution, 1775–1783—Participation, Jewish—Juvenile literature. 4. Jews—United States—Biography—Juvenile literature. 5. Bankers—United States—Biography—Juvenile literature. [1. Salomon, Haym, 1740–1785. 2. Bankers. 3. Jews—United States—Biography. 4. United States—History—Revolution, 1775–1783.]
I. Title. II. Series.
  E302.6.S17 A83 2004
  973.3'092—dc21

                                                    2002152074

# CONTENTS

# 1. The Early Years

On September 15, 1776, the British army, under the command of Sir William Howe, captured the city of New York. Although many of the citizens who were loyal to the American fight for independence fled, a young Jewish immigrant from Poland returned to the war-torn city from Lake George. Haym Salomon had left the city to bring desperately needed supplies to General Philip Schuyler's Continental army. Upon his return, Salomon would remain in the British-held New York City and secretly help imprisoned patriots escape from the British prison.

Haym Salomon had come to New York as a poor immigrant. Within a few short years, he rose to become one of the great financiers of the American Revolution. Without Salomon's fluency in more than seven languages and his ability to buy and sell foreign currency, Robert Morris, the superintendent of finance for the

---

*Opposite*: Shown is a portrait of Haym Salomon. The Jews who came to America were grateful for the freedom they found. In 1790, Rabbi Moses Seixas said to George Washington, "Deprived as we heretofore have been of the invaluable rights of free citizens, we now . . . behold a government . . . which to bigotry gives no sanction . . ."

Continental Congress, would have had a difficult time meeting the heavy financial demands of the American Revolution. By 1782, Haym Salomon would become the official broker for the United States of America.

• • • • •

Haym Salomon was born in 1740, in present-day Lissa, Poland. Haym was brought up in a family of devout Jews. In the late fifteenth century, Haym's ancestors had fled Portugal because the Inquisition demanded that all Jews convert to Catholicism. The Salomons, along with thousands of other Jewish families, settled in Poland where centuries before Casimir III, the king of Poland, had invited Jews to live. These Jewish immigrants founded their first synagogue in Lissa by 1626.

In Haym's village there were many other Jewish families. As the Jews of Eastern Europe usually lived in villages with other Jews, they developed their own language, which was called Yiddish. Although Haym studied the basics of Hebrew and obtained some elementary education, he never learned to write in Yiddish.

In 1764, Stanislaw August Poniatowski was elected to the throne of Poland and Lithuania with the strong

*Opposite*: In 1772, the powerful nations of Russia, Prussia, and Austria began partitioning, or dividing, the lands of Poland for themselves. Thomas Kitchin's 1773 map depicts the claims these nations made on Polish territory.

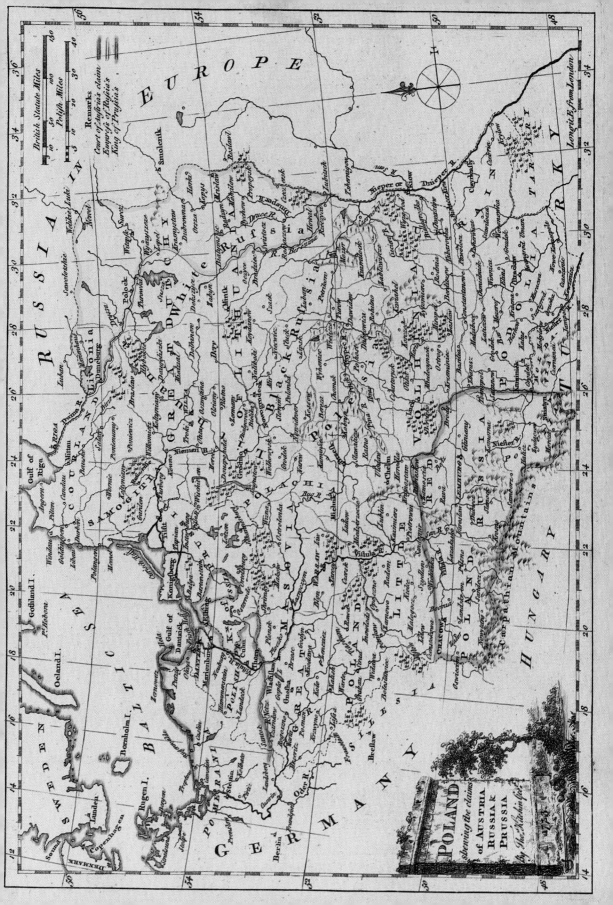

POLAND shewing the claims of AUSTRIA RUSSIA & PRUSSIA

In this engraving of an eighteenth-century Portuguese synagogue,
a rabbi holds the Torah, or the Jewish Bible, aloft before reading
a passage from this Scripture to his congregation. Originally
drawn by J. Buys, the image was later engraved and etched
by the artist C. Philips Jacobszoon around 1781.

support of Catherine the Great of Russia. Under his
brief reign, Stanislaw strengthened the power of the
monarchy. Unfortunately, his government instituted a
tax on Jewish families. The financial hardships
caused by this extra tax forced Salomon to leave his
family in his early twenties. Once Salomon left, his
family would have one less person to feed. Salomon
traveled around Europe, searching for a country that
encouraged education and religious freedom and that
allowed its people a voice in the ways in which the

Stanislaw August Poniatowski II reigned, with the consent
of Catherine II of Russia, as king of Poland between 1764
and 1795. His subjects paid a tax based on the number of
chimneys in their home. Jews paid 30 piastres for each
chimney, while non-Jews paid only 6 piastres. This 1802
portrait of the king was created by Élizabeth Vigée-Lebrun.

government formed its policies. Salomon was unable to find such a country in Europe.

During Salomon's travels, he learned to speak seven languages: English, Spanish, French, Italian, Russian, German, and Polish. He also learned how to exchange money from one country's currency to another's with ease. Salomon left Europe still searching for a land where the important ideal of freedom would be honored. He hoped he might find such a world in the British colonies, which had a reputation for being tolerant. Most scholars believe that Haym Salomon arrived in New York City in 1772, but his name has been found on a document dating from 1764, recorded in a receipt book owned by the New York merchants Judah and Moses M. Hays.

In 1764, the New York colony was reeling under British pressure to pay for the French and Indian War, which had ended in 1763. Although Britain had defeated the French, the British wanted the colonists to pay additional taxes to cover Britain's heavy debt from the war. The New York Assembly, a colonial legislative body, responded in anger, noting that taxes should not be levied against the colonists without their consent. They went as far as to say that their liberty was at stake. A group of men who called themselves the Liberty Boys began to meet in New York. Haym Salomon was a member of this group. The Liberty Boys sent a petition to King George III asking the king that the colonies be granted the right to tax themselves.

Parliament ignored the pleas from the colonists and passed the Stamp Act and the Quartering Act in 1765. The Stamp Act required that a stamp be purchased and placed on all printed materials, such as newspapers, pamphlets, legal documents, and playing cards, to show that the tax had been paid. The colonists were furious. Effigies, or dummies that resembled British agents, were

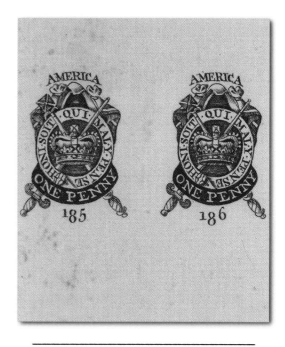

This is a close-up of a 1765 proof sheet of official stamps. The stamps were to be attached to documents such as newspapers and pamphlets. Resistance to the Stamp Act was so great that few documents bearing the stamp have survived.

burned in Massachusetts and New York. The Liberty Boys, under the leadership of Isaac Sears, John Lamb, and Alexander MacDougall, protested in the streets of New York. They eventually joined forces with a larger group that was spreading throughout the colonies, called the Sons of Liberty. Under the pressure of these politically active groups, as well as that of journalists and the various governing bodies of each colony, England repealed the Stamp Act in March 1766. England was still faced with the same problem of debt,

This 1770 drawing of the liberty pole in New York was created by P. E. Du Simitière. The barracks of the British soldiers in New York were near the liberty pole. The soldiers resented this public display of colonial resistance and cut down the pole, only to see it rebuilt by the patriots.

however, and the Quartering Act, which demanded that the colonists give room and board to British soldiers, remained in effect.

Charles Townshend, chancellor of the exchequer, comparable to a present-day U.S. secretary of the treasury, convinced Parliament to enact new taxes on tea, glass, and paper. These taxes became known as the Townshend Acts. In response, Samuel Adams, a Boston patriot and founder of the Sons of Liberty, called for the colonists to boycott, or refuse to buy, all English goods.

In reaction to the boycott, the British cut down the liberty pole in New York City. The liberty pole was a place where the New York Sons of Liberty gathered to discuss the latest British outrage. A riot broke out, and British soldiers struck men with their bayonets. Although several New Yorkers and British soldiers were wounded, no one was killed. By March 5, 1770, all the Townshend Acts, except for the tax on tea, were repealed. The damage between Britain and the colonies, however, could not be repaired.

Parliament then gave the struggling British East India Company the sole right to sell tea directly to the colonies. Although the price of British tea would then be lower for the colonists, they still resented this interference in their colonial trade. The Sons of Liberty decided to destroy the East India Company's tea. On December 16, 1773, the Sons of Liberty dumped 342 tea chests into Boston's harbor in what became known as the Boston Tea Party.

King George fought back by demanding that Parliament pass a series of acts that were known in England as the Coercive Acts, and in the colonies as the Intolerable Acts. The port of Boston was closed until the East India Company was paid for the tea that had been destroyed, which meant that no colonial ships could enter or leave the harbor. The colony of Massachusetts, which included the city of Boston, was placed under British military rule. British soldiers stayed in colonists'

*The following Perſons are nominated by the Sons of Liberty, to repreſent them in the Committee, for the City and County of New-York.*

1 ISAAC LOW,
2 Philip Livingſton,
3 James Duane,
4 John Alſop,
5 John Jay,
6 Peter V. B. Livingſton,
7 Iſaac Sears,
8 David Johnſon,
9 Alexander M'Dougall,
10 Thomas Randal,
11 Leonard Liſpenard,
12 John Broome
13 Joſeph Hallett,
14 Nicholas Hoffman,
15 Abraham Walton,
16 Henry Remſen,
17 Peter T. Curtenius,
18 Abraham Braſher,
19 Abraham P. Lott,
20 Abraham Duryee,
21 Francis Lewis,
22 Joſeph Totten,
23 Thomas Ivers,
24 Hercules Mulligan,
25 John Anthony,
26 Francis Baſſet,
27 Victor Bicker,
28 John White,
29 Theophilus Anthony,
30 William Goforth,
31 William Denning,
32 Iſaac Rooſevelt,
33 Jacob Van Voorhees,
34 Jeremiah Platt,

35 Comfort Sands,
36 Robert Benſon,
37 William W. Gilbert,
38 Nicholas Rooſevelt,
39 Edward Fleming,
40 Lawrence Embree,
41 Samuel Jones,
42 Frederick Jay,
43 William W. Ludlow,
44 John B. Moore,
45 Rudolphus Ritzema,
46 Lindley Murray,
47 Lancaſter Burling,
48 John Laſher,
49 George Janaway,
50 James Beekman,
51 Samuel Verplanck,
52 Richard Yates,
53 David Clarkſon,
54 Thomas Smith,
55 James Desbroſſes,
56 Benjamin Kiſſam,
57 John M. Scott,
58 Cornelius Clopper,
59 John Reade,
60 John Van Cortlandt,
61 Jacobus Van Zandt,
62 Gerardus Duyckinck,
63 Thomas Marſton,
64 John Morton,
65 Richard Sharpe,
66 Abraham Brinckerhoff,
67 Walter Franklin,

68 Evert Banker,
69 Robert Ray,
70 Nicholas Bogart, *Broad Way.*
71 John Lamb,
72 Daniel Phœnix,
73 Anthony Van Dam,
74 Daniel Dunſcomb,
75 Lewis Pintard,
76 Cornelius P. Low,
77 Peter Byvanck,
78 George Foliot,
79 Theodorus Van Wyck,
80 John Woodward,
81 John W. Smith,
82 Wynant Kettletaſs,
83 John Pell,
84 Luke Van Ranſt,
85 Peter Vandervoort,
86 Peter Clopper,
87 John Imlay,
88 Garret Abeel,
89 Peter Pra Van Zandt,
90 Capt. William Hyer,
91 Thomas Tucker,
92 Jacob Le Roy,
93 Richard Deane,
94 Capt. Nicholas Bogart,
95 David Beekman
96 William Bedlow,
97 William Poſt, Painter.
98 Iſaac Stoutenburgh,
99 Andrew Marſchalk,
100 Peter Meſſier.

NEW-YORK, April 28, 1775.

## TO THE PUBLIC.

AT a Meeting of a great Number of the Inhabitants of this City, at the Liberty Pole, Yeſterday Afternoon, the following Nomination of Deputies, to ſerve in Provincial Congreſs, was unanimouſly agreed to, viz.

Leonard Liſpenard,
Iſaac Rooſevelt,
Gabriel W. Ludlow,
Peter Van Brugh Livingſton,
John Broome,
David Clarkſon,
Alexander M'Dougall,

William Bedlow,
Iſaac Sears,
Thomas Smith,
John M. Scott,
John Woodward,
Hugh Hughes,
John Van Cortlandt,

John W. Smith,
Peter T. Curtenius,
Jacobus Vanzandt,
Peter Vandervoort,
Samuel Broome,
Peter Clopper.

The Sons of Liberty posted this broadside on April 28, 1775, to announce the nomination of deputies to the provincial congress. This congress legislated New York's laws and provided funds and men to fight the war once the colonies rebelled against British rule.

homes, by decree. Also, as part of these acts, if a British soldier injured a colonist in the line of duty, the soldier was to be tried in England, not in the colonies.

These Coercive Acts motivated the thirteen colonies to unite. In Massachusetts, Samuel Adams declared, "But what else could have been expected from a Parliament too long under the dictates and controul of an Administration which seems to be totally lost to all sense and feeling of morality, and governed by passion, cruelty and revenge?" In Pennsylvania, resolutions were passed in an effort to support Boston, and, on March 23, 1775, in the Virginia House of Burgesses, Patrick Henry cried, "Is life so dear or peace so sweet as to be purchased at the price of chains and slavery? . . . I know not what course others may take but as for me, give me liberty or give me death!" The patriots were prepared to die for the freedom they sought, and Haym Salomon, as a member of the Sons of Liberty, was one of them.

# 2. The Revolution Begins

By 1775, Haym Salomon was a busy merchant in New York City. Most colonial merchants sold clothing, food, and drink. They traded their goods with England, Scotland, Ireland, France, Spain, and Holland, as well as with countries as far away as Turkey and China. To these countries merchants exported products such as tobacco, grain, indigo, furs, lumber, soft coal, and tar. Most merchants kept shop in their own homes. The street level was used for business, and the merchant's family lived upstairs. In their shops merchants sold fine fabrics, Brussels lace, pearl necklaces, coffee, sugar, and chocolate. Merchants such as Salomon were highly respected within colonial society. They could sell goods at a fair price and still make a small profit.

Merchants purchased local goods from farmers or from ship captains who arrived from foreign ports. Sometimes they paid for the items they wanted to buy, and occasionally they would barter, exchanging a local product for exotic spices and unusual products such as

This reconstructed mid-eighteenth-century colonial shop is part of Colonial Williamsburg, a museum that specializes in period recreations from the eighteenth century. The layout and contents of the shop are typical of a merchant shop in the 1700s. The products on the display counter are packaged and labeled exactly as they would have been in colonial times.

pickled limes, citron, sweet oil, figs, olives, raisins, and gold and silver.

A merchant's shop was a main center of social activity during colonial times. According to author James Shouler, a merchant's "influence was great, for he knew every one; and at his store, as in a tavern, men drew up by the fire to discuss politics and the local news, stimulated by the glass of liquor which he disdained not to measure out for modest coin." In Haym Salomon's shop, the news of the Battle of Lexington and Concord, which took place on April 19, 1775, must have shaken every New Yorker who came in the door.

On April 18, 1775, the British general Gage had sent seven hundred soldiers to Concord, Massachusetts, to take the weapons that were stored there. Paul Revere, William Dawes, and Dr. Samuel Prescott rode between Boston and Concord to warn colonists that the British soldiers were marching toward them. As a result of that midnight ride, the local militiamen gathered on the green in the center of Lexington at dawn on April 19. The British major John Pitcairn ordered the militia to disperse but a shot was fired. This shot began the American Revolution. By the end of the day, after fighting in Lexington, in Concord, and on the road back to Boston, 73 British soldiers had been killed, 174 were wounded, and 26 were missing. The Americans suffered losses as well. There were 49 men killed, and 42 others were wounded. Both sides retreated to tend to their

*The Battle of Lexington Green* was created by Amos Doolittle, an engraver and silversmith, in 1775. The engagement of British troops and American militia at Lexington, Massachusetts, resulted in eighteen American casualties. This was the first battle of the American Revolution.

wounded and to bury their dead. A war for independence from King George had begun. As the news began to reach New York City, Haym Salomon decided that he had to do something to help this great American cause.

# 3. The Battle for the North Country

In colonial America, the North Country included the British colonies of Canada, the northern territory of Vermont and Maine, and the regions of present-day New Hampshire and northern New York. During the winter of 1775, Colonel Henry Knox headed an expedition for the Americans to move fifty-nine cannons from Fort Ticonderoga, located on the northern tip of Lake George, to Boston, Massachusetts, which was then under British control. His troops dragged the cannons overland and positioned them on Dorchester Heights, which overlooked Boston. The cannons were so menacing as they faced down upon the city that Lieutenant General William Howe and his forces fled the city. General George Washington, the recently appointed commander in chief of the new Continental army, was then in control of Boston and its harbor.

General Washington ordered General Richard Montgomery, Colonel Benedict Arnold, and Ethan Allen to carry out a two-pronged attack to capture the British-held Canadian city of Quebec. As the men drew up plans for their attack on Quebec, General Philip Schuyler was gathering supplies for their expedition, frantically building boats, and desperately searching for provisions, food, and clothes for the recruits at Fort Ticonderoga.

Salomon and the Sons of Liberty in New York waited anxiously for information concerning the assault on Quebec. As the long winter of 1775 turned to 1776, Salomon learned that the first part of General Richard Montgomery's attack on the

"Not a moment's time is to be lost in the preparation for this enterprise," wrote George Washington to General Philip Schuyler, shown here, as Schuyler readied for the invasion of Quebec. Jacob Lazarus created this 1881 portrait from an earlier work done by John Trumbull.

city of Montreal had gone well. Unfortunately, the news concerning Colonel Benedict Arnold's expedition through the wilderness of Maine was grim. Almost half of the one thousand men who had left with Colonel Arnold died before they reached the St. Lawrence River. The Continental soldiers were not well clothed, their shoes and boots fell apart, their blankets were wet and rotted, and their food had gone bad. Arnold's men who did survive joined Montgomery's forces on December 1, 1775. The American troops gathered

*The Death of General Montgomery in the Attack on Quebec, December 31, 1775* was painted by John Trumbull in 1786. General Richard Montgomery had been a British officer who had switched allegiance to join the American fight for independence.

outside the walls of Quebec, waiting for orders to attack the city.

Weeks after the events took place, Salomon learned that, on the dawn of December 31, 1775, the two-pronged attack had finally been launched during a fierce snowstorm. Montgomery was killed as he stormed the gates of Quebec, and Benedict Arnold was shot in the leg at the barricades of the city's Lower Town. Arnold did not surrender, however. He laid siege outside the great fortress. As the winter snows began to melt and the ice on the St. Lawrence River thawed, British reinforcements arrived at Quebec. Many of the two thousand Americans under Arnold's command were suffering from and dying of smallpox. The healthy soldiers were weak from a lack of food, as their diet consisted mainly of cornmeal. Benedict Arnold and General William Thompson, who had arrived with American reinforcements, realized they must begin a hasty retreat.

As Salomon listened to the stories of the soldiers in Quebec who had no boots, no shoes, no warm blankets, and not enough food, he realized that a merchant with access to all these items could do something important to help. As a seller of goods, he could purchase supplies, transport them to the Continental army, and then set up his tent and offer these goods for sale to the troops. Salomon closed his business in New York City and gathered many of the items that the soldiers needed. He climbed on his wagon, which was loaded with provisions, and took the Post Road to Albany in upstate New York.

In June 1776, Salomon met with Leonard Gansevoort, a lawyer and a leader of the Whig, or pro-independence, political party in Albany. Salomon told Gansevoort that he was eager to support the American cause and that he was prepared to bring the desperately needed goods to the soldiers at Fort Ticonderoga. He asked Gansevoort to recommend him to General

*Provisions in Sight!* was drawn by Denman Fink and engraved by F. H. Wellington for publication in the February 1903 issue of the illustrated magazine *The Century*. Benedict Arnold's starving troops, traveling along the Chaudière River on their way to Quebec, joyfully spot a patriot arriving with food and supplies.

f

f

f

f

f

f

f

f

f

f

f

f

f

f

*Juts*

*Carrillon*

*Well*

b

b

b

b

b

b

c

Schuyler, and Gansevoort agreed. Gansevoort knew that Salomon was one of the Sons of Liberty, and he wrote to Schuyler that Salomon was a man that they could trust:

> *New York, June 12th, 1776*
>
> *Hon'd Sir,*
>
> *I am just this Moment arrived here and have not yet heard the News.*
>
> *The Bearer hereof, Mr. Haym Salomon, tells me he has laid in Stores to go Suttling [peddling among the soldiers] to Lake George, and has been informed that the General admits none, but such as have a certificate of their being friendly to our measures, to suttle there.*
>
> *I can inform the General that Mr. Salomon has hitherto sustained the character of being warmly attached to America.*
>
> *I am in great haste, dear General,*
>
> *Your very humble servant,*
>
> *Leonard Gansevoort*
>
> *The Hon'ble General Schuyler*

Salomon outfitted his wagon with more provisions and set out on the difficult journey to Lake George. He arrived at Fort Ticonderoga just as the bruised and battered American forces returning from Quebec were stumbling

---

*Previous page:* The French fort Carillon was renamed Fort Ticonderoga in 1759, after the British captured the fort from the French during the French and Indian War. This map of the fort and the surrounding area was drawn by Michel Capitaine du Chesnoy in 1777.

back into the fort. Many of these men were suffering from smallpox, dysentery, and tuberculosis.

When Salomon arrived at Lake George, he set up a tent that was probably no more than 6 square feet (.55 sq m) and 5 feet high (.46 sq m). He presented his letter from Gansevoort to General Philip Schuyler. The general was grateful that Salomon had arrived with provisions for the soldiers. Within a sutler's tent, the soldiers could purchase coats, trousers, wool socks, caps, shirts, shoes, boots, and overcoats. They could buy woolen blankets and buttons. They found sewing kits, pipes, and muskets. Salomon might also have carried bayonets, rifles with powder horns and hunting bags to hold the

*A sutler was a merchant who sold his goods to soldiers at forts, posts, and encampments. He set up a large tent and each month the sutler was charged a fee per soldier for the right to sell his goods. This rent went to widows' and orphans' funds and to soldiers' pensions. Sutlers sold food, clothes, coffee, tobacco, blankets, pots and pans, sewing items, knives, axes, shovels, medicine, and weapons and ammunition. The sutler could sell only a half-pint of liquor to each soldier per day. After the American Revolution, many sutlers opened general stores. These stores often served as meeting places for settlers, especially in remote villages. Trappers and traders often brought their furs to sutlers and would use the furs to trade for the essential items they needed to survive in the woods.*

This Revolutionary War–era canteen was typical of those carried by Continental soldiers and was made of wood and iron.

horns, lead balls, and extra flint. The soldiers could buy axes to cut badly needed lumber, and canteens and cups to hold liquids to satisfy their thirst. Salomon also brought fire-starting kits, which contained flint and steel tinderboxes, candles and candleholders made of brass and wrought iron, and lanterns. Soldiers could also purchase iron pots for cooking campfires, wooden plates called trenchers, eating utensils, and iron forks with two tongs for picking up the food from a campfire.

To help the men stay well groomed, Salomon probably carried razors, scissors, hair curlers made of clay, and combs made of brass. Reading spectacles, which came in small wooden boxes and which were held in place with ribbon, were also available. The soldiers tried them on in order to find a pair that would correct their sight. For rest and relaxation, soldiers could buy tobacco, writing paper, and brass stamps and wax to seal their letters.

Salomon's sutler's tent was also a place where local farmers could bring flour, meat, fish, vegetables, berries, and maple syrup. The army's ration of 1 pound (.45 kg) of flour and meat per day did not provide for such delicacies. The soldiers could use their pay to supplement the army diet, to purchase warm clothes, and to buy leather shoes and boots for their blistered, bleeding feet.

Haym Salomon's provisions came just in time, for, during that summer of 1776, Benedict Arnold and his men were feverishly building the first fleet of American ships in order to stop the British advance down Lake Champlain, once again under the command of Sir Guy Carleton. This time Carleton sailed down Lake Champlain with twenty-nine vessels.

The American soldiers prepared to meet his attack by building America's first naval fleet. More than two hundred men were in the North Country constructing gondolas and bateaux. On October 11, Benedict Arnold and an American fleet of about sixteen ships finally faced the British navy at the southern tip of Valcour Island on Lake Champlain and a fiery battle began.

By the end of the day the British had the upper hand and had formed a line between New York's shore and the southern tip of Valcour Island, certain that they had trapped what was left of the American fleet. That night, however, under the cover of heavy fog, the Americans sailed close to the shore and slipped past the British warships. When the British awoke the next morning, the American fleet was gone.

The British pursued the Americans, and, on October 13, the two fleets engaged in another battle. After five

This watercolor by C. Randle, created around 1776, depicts the October 11, 1776, Battle of Valcour Island. Before the battle, Benedict Arnold, knowing his fleet was outnumbered, strategized the placement of his ships, which the artist has depicted in this painting. When the battle began, the movement of the British fleet was slowed by heavy winds. The Americans, however, were able to use the wind to their advantage.

hours of fighting, the Americans burned what remained of their fleet rather than see their ships fall into the hands of the British. The Americans then fled on foot to Fort Ticonderoga where they braced themselves for the onslaught of the British army. General Carleton, however, could feel the chill of the approaching winter and turned his fleet back toward the safety of Quebec, rather than risk having his ships trapped when the northern lakes froze. Carleton believed that he could destroy what was left of the ragged American army in the spring.

Before Salomon knew the outcome of the Battle of Lake Champlain, he was already on his way back to New York City. Word had come that General William Howe and his brother, Admiral Richard Howe, were about to attack New York City. Salomon left Fort Ticonderoga and raced south to his beloved city, hoping to be of aid to his brothers in arms, the Sons of Liberty. Salomon's role in the struggle for liberty had only just begun.

# 4. A Rebel with a Cause

The colonists considered it a great victory when General Carleton turned his fleet around and retreated to Quebec. The Americans badly needed a victory, as General Washington's army had suffered terrible defeats on Long Island and in New York City.

British lieutenant general William Howe was forced to leave Boston in early March 1776. He then took over Staten Island on July 2, 1776. Admiral Richard Howe followed him to New York with a second fleet. On August 27, William Howe attacked General Washington and his army in what came to be known as the Battle of Long Island. Both armies lost more than 400 men, and 1,200 Americans were taken prisoner. Washington retreated with his remaining men silently and swiftly on the night of August 29 to the northern part of New York City. By October 21, Washington and his army had fallen back to White Plains.

Howe and his troops followed Washington. After the Battle of White Plains, Washington's elusive army slipped again from Howe's grasp and crossed the

Franz Xaver Habermann created this 1776 hand-colored etching, which depicts the arrival of British troops in New York City in September 1776. British general Howe had gathered approximately twenty-five thousand British soldiers to take over New York.

Hudson River to join General Nathanael Greene and his men in New Jersey. The Americans continued to withdraw until they finally crossed the Delaware River and regrouped in Pennsylvania.

Salomon returned to New York City just days before Howe took control on September 15. British soldiers were soon swarming on every street, looking to arrest rebel soldiers and spies. On September 21, a warehouse on Whitehall Slip in the lower part of Manhattan was set on fire. The blaze was fanned by wild winds, and the

fire burned most of lower Manhattan and engulfed Trinity Church. The fire was finally stopped in an open field at King's College, which adjoined Trinity Church. The British suspected that the Sons of Liberty had started the fire. British officer Captain Frederick Mackenzie wrote in his diary, "During the time the Rebels were in possession of the town, many of them were heard to say they would burn it, sooner than it should become a nest for Tories."

British soldiers gathered the rebels they believed had started the blaze, shot some suspects on the spot, and arrested others. As a well-known member of the Sons of Liberty, Salomon was arrested by Major General Robertson and taken to a makeshift prison called the Old Sugar House. The building was in ruins. The roof had fallen apart, and whenever it rained the prisoners became soaked. More men died from diseases such as dysentery, typhus, tuberculosis, and cholera than they did from execution by the British. In this prison, Salomon developed a severe cough that plagued him for the rest of his life.

Salomon did not remain in this jail for long. He was transferred to an even deadlier place, the Bridewell Prison. William Cunningham was the provost, or the official, who ran this prison. As Cunningham often

*Previous spread*: The September 21, 1776, fire in New York City destroyed about five hundred homes, about one-quarter of the city. Franz Xaver Habermann created this 1776 engraving of the inferno.

tortured his prisoners, the prison became known as the Provost Prison. The Provost had originally been constructed as a debtors prison and workhouse. It was made of dark gray stone and was one of the few buildings in lower Manhattan that survived the horrific fire. The cells were so packed with prisoners that, when they slept on the wooden boards, the men all had to turn at the same time. Salomon was probably grateful not to be called out of the cell, however. When a prisoner was taken out, he was usually tortured. Salomon ate his moldy bread and drank the thin soups and foul water that were offered.

The British forces in New York crowded their American prisoners of war into private homes, barns, churches, sugar houses, and debtors prisons, such as the Provost, shown here in an engraving. After two fires destroyed many of these locales, prisoners were also held on ships.

During his imprisonment, Salomon met several Hessian officers, who were guarding the prisoners. These officers spoke of Salomon's fluency in German and other languages to Lieutenant General Heister, a German officer serving under the British command.

A man who could speak so many languages would be useful to Heister, and it is likely that Heister arranged for Salomon's parole. Heister appointed Salomon and Tory merchant William Tongue as purveyors of goods. This meant that they would purchase goods for the British prison. Once Salomon was released from prison on parole, both Heister and Tongue carefully observed his actions.

Tongue and Salomon did more than just purchase goods for the prison. They also established a merchant broker's office in Hanover Square. A broker bought and sold money from foreign countries and then exchanged it for British money. Salomon's experience as a merchant and a sutler, as well as his knowledge of foreign languages and currency, served him well. An advertisement for their office was placed in the *New-York Gazette* and the *Weekly Mercury* on September 30, 1776:

> *A Merchant Broker's Office and*
> *Auction or Public Vendue Room*
> *is opened by William Tongue. . . .*
> *having the supply of his Majesty's*
> *guards, and the Hessian officers . . .*

This portrait of John Ulrich Zeth, a young Hessian soldier, was painted around 1777 by Friedrich Konstantin von Germann. The Hessians who fought for the British during the American Revolution were mercenaries, which meant that they fought solely for money and not for a political cause. However, it was the Hessian rulers in Europe who profited the most from the services of their soldiers.

In prison Salomon had also met Monsieur Samuel Demezes, a French prisoner. Because Demezes was French, Provost Cunningham took great pleasure in frequently dragging him out of the cell to torture him. When Salomon was released, he vowed to secure the freedom of this man who had endured Cunningham's cruelties.

Both Salomon and Demezes secretly helped American and French soldiers escape from the Provost. As Salomon was providing goods for the Hessian soldiers who guarded the prisoners, he developed an acquaintance with some of these men. Salomon was able to persuade a few Hessians to look the other way while prisoners made their escape. Salomon knew that many of the young German guards served in the Hessian army solely for the money and had no loyalty to the British. Salomon covertly met with younger German soldiers who were dissatisfied with the British army. He convinced them to take advantage of the land grants that the state of Pennsylvania was offering. Pennsylvania was giving 100 acres (40 ha) of land to Hessian soldiers who left the British army. Although many of the older Hessians would not consider the offer because they could be shot if they were caught, a good number of the younger men took that risk and deserted.

Meanwhile, Salomon had become so invaluable to the British that they eventually released him from his probation. As most of the Jewish citizens of New York City were patriots and had fled New York with the

British invasion, Salomon didn't have many friends left in the hostile city. People faithful to the cause wondered suspiciously how Salomon had secured his release from the Provost. The Tories also did not trust him because he was a known member of the Sons of Liberty. However, Salomon continued to help French and American prisoners escape from the prison and to persuade Hessian soldiers to desert. During the day, Salomon offered his services as a merchant, a ship's chandler, a distiller, and an interpreter.

On December 26, 1776, George Washington engaged in his first successful battle. The Continental army claimed Trenton, New Jersey, and then on January 3, 1777, the Americans took Princeton, New Jersey.

When word of the American Revolution reached Europe, many of the wealthy noblemen were astounded by the colonists' audacity to revolt against one of the world's strongest powers. Although this made some noblemen nervous, these early American victories won the respect of other noblemen. In 1777, the nineteen-year-old Frenchman Marquis de Lafayette decided to join the American forces, bringing with him not only a considerable amount of money, but also the power and prestige of his noble position. Lafayette had a direct tie to Louis XVI, king of France. This came as welcome news to George Washington, who wanted to secure an alliance with France, Britain's formidable enemy. France and England had a history of territorial disputes, the most recent being their colonial claims to lands of North America during the French and Indian War, which lasted from 1754 to 1763.

The Americans were desperate for men who could speak some of the many different languages of these new European allies. They also needed men who had some understanding of foreign currency because money, in the form of contributions and loans, that came in from Europe would need to be properly exchanged. Haym Salomon filled both of these descriptions.

# 5. Marriage, Family, and a Narrow Escape

In 1777, Haym Salomon was thirty-seven years old and owned a small but profitable merchant shop. He had done so well that he was able to move his office from 222 Broad Street to 245 Broad Street, which put him closer to the New York City business district. During this time he continued to help prisoners escape, hiding some of them in his own home. Salomon also fell in love with Rachel Franks. She was the fifteen-year-old daughter of a Jewish tailor, Moses Benjamin Franks, and his wife Bilhah Abigail. Rachel agreed to marry Haym in spite of the twenty-one-year difference in their ages. Because they had the financial means to support a

Records from the New York Provincial Congress of July 30, 1776, note that a "Hyam Solomon, the distiller" acted as a translator for a "Doctor Joseph Gerreau, a Frenchman." Salomon, above, was sketched by an unknown artist.

According to Jewish law a *ketubah* is a marriage contract that details how a husband shall financially provide for his wife. A partial translation of this document states "Hayim, the son of Shelomo said to the maiden Rachel, the daughter of Moshe Franks: 'Be thou my wife according to the law of Moses and Israel. . . .'"

family, older, well-established gentlemen often married younger women in colonial times. On July 6, 1777, Abraham I. Abrahams, a leader of the Jewish Congregation Shearith Israel, officiated the ceremony.

Congregation Shearith Israel is the oldest Jewish congregation in America. Twenty-three Jews had come to New York from Brazil to form a permanent congregation in 1654. These Jews had been living in the Dutch colony in Recife, Brazil, and had narrowly escaped the Inquisition when the Portuguese captured Recife that year. The Jewish immigrants made their way by ship to New York City. When they arrived, Peter Stuyvesant

This commemorative plate is decorated with an illustration of Shearith Israel, depicting where the congregation met from 1730 until 1817. Shearith Israel was the only Jewish congregation in New York City until 1825. Early members helped to found both King's College, which later became Columbia University, and the New York Stock Exchange.

was the Dutch colonial governor of New Amsterdam. The city became New York when it was acquired later by the British in 1664. Stuyvesant did not want the Jews to settle in his colony, but he was ordered by the Dutch West India Company to accept the Jewish colonists from Brazil. The Jews then established Shearith Israel, the same congregation to which Rachel and Haym belonged.

The family of Rachel's mother, Bilhah Abigail, had been in the colonies for more than eighty years. Asser Levy van Swellem, Rachel's great grandfather, and Jacob Barsimson had petitioned Governor Peter Stuyvesant for the right to stand guard against Indian attacks.

Two of Rachel's uncles, David Franks and Nathan Levy, were successful businessmen. The two men formed the Levy and Franks Company, which had many ships, including the *Myrtilla*. This ship carried the Liberty Bell, the American symbol of freedom, from England to Philadelphia in 1752. The Liberty Bell had been ordered by the Pennsylvania Assembly in order to proclaim liberty whenever it was rung. Inscribed on the bell was a biblical verse from Lev. 25.10, which states, "Proclaim Liberty thro'all the Land to all the Inhabitants thereof." Although the older David Franks sided with the British during the war, his two nephews, Isaac and David Salisbury Franks, were patriots.

By 1777, the year that Haym and Rachel were married, British general Howe was desperate to crush the

American rebellion. In an effort to end the war, General Howe had left New York City, leaving General Henry Clinton in charge. Howe intended to strike the rebels at the heart of their government, the Continental Congress in Philadelphia, Pennsylvania. Howe believed that the rebel army would collapse if Philadelphia were under British control. General Howe sailed to Chesapeake Bay in Maryland and marched between sixteen thousand and eighteen thousand soldiers to Elkton,

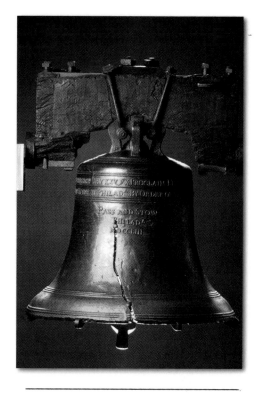

The Liberty Bell was first cast in London in 1752 by the Whitechapel Bell Foundry. Since the bell cracked when it was first rung in Philadelphia, the bell was melted down and recast, twice, until both the form and tone of the bell were satisfactory.

Maryland, just south of Philadelphia. George Washington and about eleven thousand Continental soldiers met Howe's army at Brandywine where the Battle of Brandywine Creek was fought. American casualties numbered more than one thousand men in one of the worst American defeats of the war. Washington retreated, and Howe marched into Philadelphia on September 26, 1777. After another battle and defeat at Germantown, Washington retreated

General Sir William Howe commanded the British army during the American Revolution between 1776 and 1778. General Washington's victories at Princeton and Trenton had surprised Howe, as Washington did not descend from nobility nor had he had any formal military training, qualifications that Howe thought necessary for leadership. C. Corbutt created this portrait in 1777.

to the winter camp at Valley Forge, Pennsylvania. General Howe enjoyed the winter in Philadelphia, certain that the American army would soon surrender.

There were, however, several major problems that General Howe did not anticipate. On October 17, 1777, the American general Horatio Gates defeated British general John Burgoyne at the Battle of Saratoga in Saratoga, New York. This American victory upset the British plan to cut the colonies in half by means of controlling the waterways of Lake Champlain, Lake George, and the Hudson River. The whole tide of the

John Ward Dunsmore created this 1907 painting, *Washington Sees the Bloody Footprints in the Snow*. General Washington and Marquis de Lafayette are on horseback inspecting the sad condition of the Continental troops at their winter camp in Valley Forge, Pennsylvania.

war had changed. As a result of this great victory, foreign governments were more willing to help finance the American Revolution.

Haym Salomon struggled to keep his business running during the war and placed advertisements in journals such as the *New-York Gazette* and the *Royal American Gazette* announcing the sale of bread, rice, wine and vinegar, silk stockings, and hats. As the Americans continued their boycott of British goods, and, as both the Americans and the British frequently captured each other's ships, it was difficult for merchants to acquire goods for trade.

Salomon began to act as a broker, or middleman, which meant that he would exchange different currencies and commodities for his customers. Merchants and farmers wanted to be paid in money that would hold its value. The currency was only good if they could use the paper money to exchange it for its face value's worth of goods. During the war most people were leery of accepting paper money, as the currency might be considered worthless when they tried to use it later in another transaction. Salomon was one of the few men in New York City who knew the value of foreign currency and who could exchange money for the correct amount in American bonds, cash, or goods. If a Frenchman, for example, had money to spend but no merchants would accept the French bills, he could go to Salomon, who would then give him the correct amount in Continental

In this September 1, 1777, lead story from the *New-York Gazette*, Sir William Howe, British general, warned smugglers of the penalties they faced should they be caught. Haym Salomon advertised his services as a merchant in this publication.

money. Salomon was able to take the French bills and exchange them with French dignitaries who were in the city for the purpose of loaning money to the American cause.

In this way the Salomons managed to survive the winter of 1777–1778. On July 20, 1778, Haym and Rachel celebrated the birth of their son, Ezekiel. By the time of Ezekiel's birth, the British had evacuated Philadelphia and the Continental Congress had returned to that city.

On August 5, 1778, another destructive fire in New York City blazed out of control. Sixty-four houses, two ships, and several shops were burned to the ground. As the fire spread along the waterfront, ammunition exploded on board the British ship, *Morning Star*. Haym knew that the British would suspect him of being involved with this fire, too.

Salomon's fears were justified. It is also possible that one of the many people that Salomon aided since he had been released from the Provost Prison gave out his name while being tortured. A prisoner might have named Salomon as one of the rebels who were helping prisoners to escape and encouraging Hessian soldiers to desert.

After the blaze was brought under control, Salomon was probably headed for home when he saw guards standing by his front door, waiting to arrest him. Salomon turned around and started off in another direction. One of the guards saw him, however, and the guards gave chase. As Salomon had long been familiar with the streets of New York, he managed to elude the soldiers in pursuit.

Unfortunately, Salomon could not go home. He realized that he would only be safe in Philadelphia. During the war, citizens needed a pass to travel on the open roads. Salomon knew where he might obtain such a pass that would permit him to make his way to Philadelphia. He traveled to Dobbs Ferry in Westchester County, where one of Salomon's friends from the Sons of Liberty, Alexander MacDougall, was stationed as a general in the Continental army. Salomon was forced to leave his wife and child behind. Had Salomon been caught a second time by the British, William Cunningham would have had Salomon hanged in the Provost Prison.

# 6. Philadelphia, the Heart of the Rebellion

Although Haym Salomon may have considered joining Alexander MacDougall's regiment upon reaching Dobbs Ferry, MacDougall knew of Salomon's talent as a sutler and a broker and probably encouraged Salomon to use those skills to help the American cause. MacDougall gave Salomon the pass he required to travel to Philadelphia. Salomon set off, taking the back roads to avoid the British regulars, who were still searching for him.

When Salomon arrived in Philadelphia, he found that the British had burned the city before they left. Merchant shops, homes, and churches were still smoldering as Salomon walked through the streets. Salomon wrote to the Continental Congress and offered his services, hoping to find employment with the government. Salomon also sought aid for his friend in the Provost Prison, Monsieur Samuel Demezes. Even though William Cunningham did not know who was helping prisoners escape from the prison, he suspected that Demezes was the inside contact.

Archibald Robertson, an artist as well as an officer in the British army, created this view of Philadelphia from the New Jersey side of the Delaware River on November 28, 1777. The British had been in control of Philadelphia since September 1777. Robertson has included himself in his depiction. He is seen drawing at the water's edge.

Salomon was afraid that if Demezes' release could not be immediately arranged, his friend might be killed. On August 25, 1778, Haym Salomon wrote to the Continental Congress:

> *To the Honorable the Continental Congress*
> *The Memorial of Haym Salomon late of the*
> *City of New York, Merchant.*
> *Humbly Sheweth,*
> *That your Memorialist [Haym Salomon]*

*was some time before the Entry of the British Troops at the said City of New York, and soon after taken up as a Spy and by General Robertson committed to the Provost — That by Interposition of Lieut. General Heister (who wanted him on account of his knowledge in the French, Polish, Russian Italian &c Languages) he was given over to the Hessian Commander who appointed him in the Commissary Way as Purveyor chiefly for the Officers — That being at New York he has been of great Service to the French & American prisoners and has assisted them with Money and helped them off to make their Escape — That this and his close connexions with such of the Hessian Officers as were inclined to resign and with Monsieur Samuel Demezes has rend[e]red him at last so obnoxious to the British Head Quarters that he was already pursued by the Guards and on Tuesday the 11th inst, he made his happy Escape from thence — This Monsieur Demezes is now most barbarously treated at the Provost's and is seemingly in danger of his life. And the Memorialist begs leave to cause him to be rememb[e]red to Congress for an exchange.*

*Your Memorialist [Haym Salomon] has upon this Event most irrecoverably lost all his Effects and Credits to the amount of Five or Six*

*thousand Pounds Sterling and left his dis-*
*tressed Wife and a Child of a Month old at New*
*York waiting that they may soon have an*
*Opportunity to come out from thence with*
*empty hands.*

*In these Circumstances he most humbly*
*prayeth to grant him any Employ in the way of*
*his Business whereby he may be enabled to sup-*
*port himself and family — And your*
*Memorialist as in duty bound &c &c*
*HAYM SALOMON*
*Philad.al Aug 25th 1778*

The Continental Congress had just returned to
Philadelphia, and the penniless Salomon did not
receive a response to his letter. Salomon turned to
Philadelphia's Jewish leaders at the Congregation
Mikveh Israel, a synagogue to which some members of
Rachel's family belonged. The head of this congregation
was Isaac Moses, one of Rachel's cousins. Influential
men from this congregation helped Salomon start a
business in Philadelphia as a merchant and a broker.
Isaac Moses was also part owner of eight merchant
ships. One of his partners was Robert Morris, who was
soon to be appointed by the Continental Congress as
the superintendent of finance.

Shortly after Salomon arrived in Philadelphia, he
arranged to have Rachel and Ezekiel join him. Salomon

*To the Honorable the Continental Congress*

*The Memorial of Hyam Solomon late of the City of New York, Merchant*

*humbly sheweth,*

That Your Memorialist was some time before the Entry of the British Troops at the said City of New York, and soon after taken up as a Spy and by General Robertson committed to the Provost — That by the Interposition of Lieut General Heister (who wanted him on account of his Knowledge in the French, Polish, Russian Italian &c.ᵃ Languages) he was given over to the Hessian Commander who appointed him in the Commissary Way as Purveyor chiefly for the Officers — That being at New York he has been of great Service to the French & American prisoners and has assisted them with Money and helped them off to make their Escape — That this and his close Connexions with such of the Hessian Officers as were inclined to resign and with Monsieur Samuel Demezes has rendred him at last so obnoxious to the British Head Quarters that he was already pursued by the Guards and on Tuesday the 11ᵗʰ inst. he made his happy Escape from th[...] — Th[...] Mon[...] Demez[...] now m[...]

---

Haym Salomon wrote this letter to the Continental Congress
on August 25, 1778. When Salomon addressed himself
as "Your Memorialist" he was acknowledging himself as
the author of a memoir, or an official letter or report.

L. Simeone created this 1984 rendering of the interior of
Congregation Mikveh Israel as it appeared in the eighteenth
century. The artist's work was based on the congregation's
detailed instructions to the carpenter and the bricklayer,
contained in the building contract, dated April 22, 1782.

opened a broker's office and a merchant business on
Front Street. One of the first men whom Salomon
approached to build up his business as a broker was
Chevalier de La Luzerne, the diplomatic ambassador for
the king of France. Luzerne was delighted to meet
Salomon, who was not only a reputable broker but also a
man with whom Luzerne could speak French. By 1779,
Salomon was the official broker for both the French con-
sulate and the office of the paymaster general. Because of
his ability to speak French, Salomon was called upon to

supply General Lafayette and his soldiers with horses, saddles, clothes, food, and weapons until French ships arrived with their own supplies. Salomon also began working for the Spanish and Dutch officials who had come to support the American Revolution and who needed to pay their own expenses until their ships could break through the British blockades.

Salomon tried to rebuild his merchant business while continuing his brokerage work for the war effort. By 1779, he was able to become part owner of a ship called the *Sally*, which would conduct trade between the colonies and Spain. Salomon's family also flourished. Around 1779, Rachel gave birth to a daughter named Sarah.

Life in Philadelphia during the war was not easy. British privateers effectively blockaded many of the ships trying to reach the colonies. This made it difficult for the French, the Spanish, and the Dutch to help the Americans. Salomon wrote a letter to a merchant in Virginia and described some of the difficulties that the merchants were facing:

> *[I will] defer sending [hats] till I hear from you. They cannot be got for less than two and a half dollars. Silk stockings are grown scarce, and am afraid I shall not be able to send you the quantity you want. Goods are grown scarce, and from the number of vessels we have lost, and our capes are now swarming with enemy cruisers, we expect they will rise considerably.*

*A privateer was an armed ship that was run and owned by private citizens. Some privateers were designed to attack enemy ships, while others were merchant ships that were capable of defending themselves in case of an attack. The ships' owners, captains, and crews also were referred to as privateers. Although privateers were not commissioned officers or sailors, they often served their countries in times of war. Privateers would attack enemy ships, capture the cargo and crew, and then set the enemy ships ablaze.*

*During the American Revolution, most of the colonial cities were close to the water, and it was easy for a captain to find young men eager for excitement and adventure at sea. The captains chose their own crews, the voyages were shorter than those in the navy, and the crew would receive a small percentage of the confiscated goods. Members of the crew served as sailors, gunners, and carpenters. They were also responsible for taking goods off the enemy ship and for watching any prisoners who were taken aboard.*

At the end of another letter to a Virginian merchant, Salomon asked that the merchant send 12,000 pounds (4,479 kg) of tobacco when the coast seemed clear of the British privateers who preyed upon the American merchant vessels.

Although Salomon was able to support his own growing family, a financial crisis arose within the American government. The Continental currency, or money, had lost much of its value and was considered almost worthless. The money could not be exchanged for goods because many merchants refused to accept it. They relied instead on bartering to run their businesses. At

This bill of exchange, made out to Haym Salomon from the Continental Loan-Office in Pennsylvania, was dated December 14, 1780. The bill specifies that Salomon is to be paid in either 400 Mexican dollars or 2,000 French livres.

this critical moment in history, Robert Morris sent for Haym Salomon. Morris hoped that Salomon could help him to build confidence in Continental money and find ways to bring more income to the struggling government. Without the money to clothe, feed, transport, and supply the army with weapons, the entire cause would die. George Washington also needed money to pay his soldiers so they would continue following him into battle. Many of the Continental soldiers had threatened to mutiny unless they were paid.

During this period, John Adams, a delegate of the Continental Congress, from Massachusetts, wrote to the Congress:

> *The art of war is so well and so equally understood by the great nations of Europe . . . that it is now generally considered as a contest of finances; so that the nation which can longest find money to carry on the war, can generally hold out the longest.*

Morris would put his trust in the Jewish broker on Front Street. It was up to Salomon to rise to the occasion.

# 7. Salomon Comes to the Aid of Morris and Washington

In 1781, George Washington appointed Robert Morris as the superintendent of finance "with the full power to raise the money needed to carry on the war." Robert Morris had left Liverpool, England, when he was fourteen years old. He settled in Philadelphia and became a prominent merchant. When his father died, Morris was left with a handsome inheritance of approximately $7,000. Morris became a shipowner and was part owner of a number of ships with Rachel Salomon's cousin Isaac Moses. Morris had originally voted against separation with England in 1776. He later signed the Declaration of Independence when the Continental Congress voted for American independence, and Morris then swore his allegiance to the new nation of the United States of America.

On June 8, 1781, according to an entry in Robert Morris's diary, Morris hired Haym Salomon to serve as his broker:

> *June 8, 1781*
> *I agreed with Mr. Haym Solomon the Broker*
> *who had been employed by the Officers of his*

C. W. Peale painted this portrait of Robert Morris around 1782. Morris, upon accepting his appointment as superintendent of finance, informed Congress, "I [will] sacrifice much of my interest, my ease, my domestic tranquility . . . the United States may command everything I have excepting my integrity; and the loss of *that* would effectually disable me from serving them more." Some congressmen feared that such a smart business man might use his new powers to advance his private interests. His skill with finances, however, made Morris the best candidate for this crucial wartime appointment.

*Most Christ[ia]n Majesty [Louis XVI, king of France] to make Sale of their Army & Navy bills, to assist me in the Sale of the Bills I am to draw for the Monies granted as Aforesaid, his Brokerage to be settled hereafter but not to exceed a half p[e]r Cent.*

In order to meet the enormous demand of funding the war, Salomon's biggest problem was to exchange the foreign currency that was arriving from European governments into American currency. For example, when the French government decided to make huge loans to

This French bill of exchange, made out to Haym Salomon, is dated June 16, 1784. The French phrase *À soixante Jours de vue* means that the check must be paid to the bearer, or owner, of the check within sixty days of it being presented to the financial institution that issued the check.

the Americans after the Battle of Saratoga, Salomon took the French money and exchanged it for American currency. As the broker for the American government, he charged a rate for performing this financial transaction. This small fee served as Salomon's salary.

Unfortunately, other brokers who did not represent the United States were giving lower exchange rates, thereby undercutting the government prices on these foreign bonds. Salomon implored local brokers to honor the government rates in order to stabilize the value of these bonds.

Salomon had to convince other American brokers that it was in their best interest for the United States of America to win the war. Life would be better for them under their self-government than under the rule of the British monarchy. Salomon also turned to the men in control of each state's finances. Each state taxed its citizens, and Salomon had to convince the treasurers that, by contributing some of that tax money to the Continental government, each state would be better served than it had been under the British monarchy. Salomon also persuaded Spain and Holland to buy American bonds.

In one example of Salomon's work, Morris noted that Salomon "informed him that Mr. Chaloner had promised not to sell under six Shillings and desired him to press the Sale of Bills. . . . I desire him [Salomon] to gain Information of the Persons the Sums the Rates to call on them and urge them to keep up the Price. . . ."

Bills of exchange are papers upon which the amount of money a person agrees to borrow from a broker or a bank is put in writing. The exact date upon which the loan will be paid is written on the bill.

Banks, from which money could be drawn, did not exist until the close of the American Revolution. Therefore, when foreign countries wished to lend the colonies money during the war, they signed bills of exchange. Brokers for the American government would calculate how much silver or gold backed the coins and paper money lent by each country. By knowing how much gold was behind a French coin, for example, countries could calculate how much money the bills of exchange were worth in terms of English pounds and American currency.

Brokers also used bills of exchange to pay off the loans the United States owed to foreign diplomats and their countries. Brokers were middlemen for these financial exchanges and received a small percentage of the transaction as payment for their services. France, Spain, and Holland gave the colonies the most financial support during the Revolution. Their loans were often made in bills of exchange.

Salomon succeeded. Local brokers decided to honor the government rates. The next morning Morris wrote, "Mr. Solomons informs me that he has Sold from Sixty to Eighty thousand Livres at 6/ on a Credit of eight Months." Each day was a constant battle to buy and sell foreign money so that it would not lose its value. This was the only way the government could secure enough money to pay its bills.

In 1781, George Washington had two major war fronts to defeat. The British were still in control of New York City under General Henry Clinton, and Lord Charles Cornwallis had just entrenched his soldiers in York-town, a small Virginian tobacco port. Cornwallis had stayed along the coast because he did not want to be trapped inland, far from British supplies that would arrive from overseas.

George Washington, shown in a portrait by Robert Edge Pime from around 1785, built large brick ovens for bread in New Jersey. He hoped this might fool British spies into thinking that the Continental army would remain near New York.

As the British generals believed that General Washington would most likely attack them in New York, Washington craftily turned his attention to General Cornwallis's army at Yorktown, Virginia. Washington met with the French general Rochambeau, and the two men decided to fool the

British into thinking that the attack was about to take place in New York City. In actuality, the Continental troops would be heading for Virginia. One major problem remained. They needed $20,000 in order to carry out this brilliant military operation. The outcome of the war depended on having the money to pay for it. Washington turned to Robert Morris for the funds to carry out this military plan. Before Washington headed to Yorktown, he wrote to Robert Morris:

> *I entreat you to procure one month's pay in specie [money] for the detachment. Part of these troops have not been paid anything for a long time past, and have on several occasions shown marks of great discontent. The service they are going upon is disagreeable to the Northern regiments: but I make no doubt that a douceur [bribe] of a little hard money would put them in proper temper.*

Morris, in turn, sent for Haym Salomon. Salomon immediately began to sell Pennsylvanian paper money to acquire silver, and he sold the foreign bills of exchange that were arriving from France, Spain, and Holland. Salomon also bought foreign currency at a low price and then sold the currency at a higher rate. By using these and similar methods, Salomon helped Morris to raise the $20,000 that Washington needed to begin the march to Virginia.

John Trumbull created these depictions of *The Surrender of Cornwallis at Yorktown*. The top painting was done in 1787 and the bottom was commissioned in 1817. When Cornwallis first broached his surrender, he sent an officer with a note and a flag of truce. Although Cornwallis later signed Washington's surrender terms, he felt too humiliated to meet with Washington and sent his deputy, General O'Hara, instead.

Washington put his plan into action. At first, he moved some of his nine thousand soldiers to Staten Island to fool Henry Clinton into thinking that he was about to attack New York. As expected, General Clinton prepared to defend it. Washington then crossed the Hudson River on August 20, 1781. He marched his men 60 miles (96.5 km) per day toward Yorktown. While Henry Clinton was still bracing for the New York attack, Washington and Rochambeau had already crossed the Delaware River. General Lafayette had the task of keeping Cornwallis's eight thousand soldiers, one-third of the British army, pinned down at Yorktown. The French fleet under Admiral Francois de Grasse had just won a sea battle in the West Indies when he received orders to sail as quickly as possible to Yorktown. De Grasse, with a fleet of about thirty warships, entered the Chesapeake Bay on August 30, about ten days before Washington and Rochambeau arrived. On September 28, the French and the Americans had Cornwallis surrounded by water and by land.

Cornwallis was trapped, outmaneuvered, and outfoxed by George Washington. On October 19, 1781, Cornwallis surrendered to the Americans. With his brilliant military strategy, help from abroad, and the backing of his financiers in Philadelphia, George Washington was able to defeat the mightiest army in the world.

There was also something to celebrate within the Salomon family as well. Haym and his family rejoiced in the birth of their daughter Deborah.

# 8. Salomon Serves a New Nation

Winning a war against Britain was an enormous task, but governing a new nation created a different set of problems that had to be overcome. It was a daunting task, particularly for the financiers. One of the first things that Robert Morris did to control the drastic swing in the value of American currency was to establish the federal Bank of North America. This bank, which opened on January 7, 1782, would handle all financial matters for the new nation. Bills from the Continental army were to be submitted to the bank and payments would then be issued. Haym Salomon was one of the first subscribers, or investors, to the bank. His faith in a national banking system encouraged other prominent men to put their money in the bank as well. This, in turn, helped to give value to the currency that the government printed. If deposits of foreign currency were made, then the government would have enough money to cover its bills. The biggest problem was giving people a sense of security so that they would deposit their money in the bank.

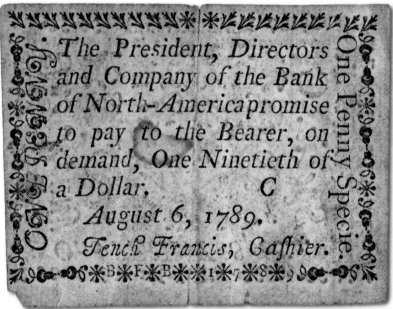

This small-change bill of credit could be redeemed for specie, or coins, by the person who possessed the bill. The Bank of North America issued this bill, shown here from the front and the back, in Philadelphia on August 6, 1789.

Salomon, as one of the first subscribers, bought two shares at $800 in specie each.

Money was desperately needed for British prisoners of war, for foreign diplomats, and for soldiers leaving the army. Various ways to make payments had to be arranged. In order to convince store owners to accept paper money, the bank guaranteed the value of the paper money that was used in exchange for goods that people wanted to buy. For example, two thousand British prisoners being held in Lancaster, York, and Frederick Town, Pennsylvania, were in desperate need of provisions. The American government had assured England that the prisoners would be well provided for and then returned to England in good condition. Without the money to purchase adequate provisions, the government could not keep its word. Salomon arranged to have British commanding officers endorse, or sign, the backs of the American money. Once the merchants who supplied the provisions were secure that banks in America and London would back these bills, the prisoners could receive the supplies they needed.

Foreign diplomats who had business in America could rely on the bank for funds. This encouraged foreign investors to do business with the new nation. An emissary of Charles III, king of Spain, needed money after the British captured his ship. Salomon made sure that the ambassador received the money he required.

*This is a partial list of the first subscribers to the Bank of North America. The Bank subscription list was completed on July 25, 1783.*

*1000 shares at $400 specie each*

| Name | Shares |
| --- | --- |
| Wm Bingham | 95 |
| John Holker | 5 |
| M. Hillegas | 1 |
| Luzerne | 1 |
| Robert Morris | 98 |
| Gouv. Morris | 1 |
| Isaac Moses | 1 |
| John Ross | 5 |
| John Swanwick | 71 |
| HAYM SALOMON | 2 |
| James Wilson | 5 |
| Thomas Willing | 11 |
| John Wilson | 2 |

France aided the Bank of North America by loaning the new nation $2,000,000. Although much of this money was used in France to cover outstanding debts for supplies that had been shipped to the United States, Morris was able to deposit approximately one quarter of that sum into the bank. This loan from France was still not enough money to cover the young country's expenses. Morris and Salomon came to the conclusion that the states would have to begin taxing their citizens in order to build up the bank reserves. Otherwise, the government money would quickly become worthless if there were no funds left to pay bills.

Robert Morris had become so dependent on Salomon that, on July 12, 1782, he gave Salomon the official title of broker to the finance office. Soon after Salomon was appointed as the official government broker, soldiers and their officers staged a rebellion and demanded payment for their services during the war.

The government owed the men $140,000 and the financial officers, which paid the government's bills, were short by $101,000. Salomon sold bills of exchange worth $37,500, but the office was still short by $60,000. Robert Morris relied upon Salomon to sell foreign bills cautiously, without flooding the market. Salomon had a talent for judging how much the market could handle. Salomon sold enough bills to raise $60,000 for the soldiers.

On January 20, 1783, the Treaty of Paris was signed, and the American Revolution was officially won. While

A broker helps people to buy and sell contracts for bills of exchange, property, or other expensive commodities. As a broker for France and for the finance office of the United States, Haym Salomon accepted paper money and bills of exchange from diplomats, foreign countries, and wealthy Americans. Salomon gave these individuals and foreign countries a receipt for their loan, or he paid them the value of the loan in American currency. This was done cautiously, for, if a country made a large loan, the value of that money would go down if it was circulated too quickly.

For example, if the United States were suddenly to print billions of American dollars today and that money flooded into our banks, the value of each dollar might drop from 100 cents per dollar to less than 100 cents per dollar. Each dollar is worth an amount of gold. As the number of dollars in circulation increases, the amount of gold representing the worth of the new bills stays the same. Therefore, each dollar is worth less gold.

Robert Morris and Haym Salomon had to hold foreign money back so this would not happen with the large loans made by France, Spain, and Holland. These loans sometimes exceeded $1,000,000. When diplomats, American soldiers, and private citizens needed to cash in their bills of exchange or wanted payment on one of their loans, they came to the broker to redeem their papers. Because the value of the money from France, Spain, and Holland changed daily, a broker needed to know exactly how much the foreign paper money was worth when it was paid in full.

Benjamin West's *Signing of the Treaty of Paris, 1782* was created before the treaty was signed in 1783. During negotiations in Paris, Benjamin Franklin insisted that he be recognized as a representative of the United States, rather than of the former British colonies. Because the British delegation refused to pose, the painting was never completed.

the citizens of the new nation celebrated in the streets, Salomon and Morris continued their job of keeping the young nation financially secure. During the summer of 1783, there was another revolt of soldiers demanding back pay. This time the soldiers marched against Congress in Philadelphia and the congressmen fled the city in fear. The soldiers were ready to riot and damage the city unless they were paid. Robert Morris himself fled, and he counted on Salomon to raise the money that was owed to the soldiers. There was so little money in the national reserves that even the Bank of North America would not allow the government to make any additional loans. This time Salomon turned to Holland and France. Salomon also convinced his relative Isaac Moses to purchase bills of exchange that were backed by Dutch guilders and French livres. With money flowing back into the bank, confidence was restored, and the soldiers accepted the government's paper money. Congress and Robert Morris returned to Philadelphia.

Not all of Salomon's financial work held such dire consequences. Many of the founding fathers came to Salomon for loans in order to pay their debts. Haym Salomon seldom charged these men any interest on these loans. James Madison wrote, "Among other members of Congress from Virginia whose resources, public and private, had been cut off, I had occasion, once, perhaps twice, myself to resort to his [Salomon's] pecuniary aid on a small scale for current wants. We regarded him as upright, intelligent, and friendly [in] his transactions with us." Thomas Jefferson, James Monroe, and James Madison all turned to Haym Salomon for financial aid. Even Robert Morris received financial help from Salomon. From abroad, Baron von Steuben was among the many foreigners who turned to Haym Salomon for loans to pay their personal bills. Although personal crises are not on a par with a national financial crisis, these great men, who relied on Salomon's generosity to keep their good name, were writing the Constitution, working in Congress, and representing the nation in foreign courts.

Great Britain antici-pated that the new American government would encounter many financial difficulties. At the end of the Revolution a Tory aristocrat named Jonathan Sewall, who had fled to Britain from the colonies, wrote to an American acquaintance, "Ah, my old friend, could you form a just idea of the immense wealth and power of the British

James Sharples did this portrait of James Madison around 1796. James Madison would serve for eight years as President Thomas Jefferson's secretary of state, and later, in 1809, Madison became the fourth president of the United States.

nation, you would tremble at the foolish audacity of your pigmy states." Sewall and other members of the British ruling class did not count on Morris and Salomon's careful handling of funds, which helped to stabilize the financial state of the young nation.

# 9. America, the First Years of the Republic

As the nation struggled to become a strong governing body, George Washington remained its commander in chief. The United States still functioned under the Articles of Confederation, which was drafted to unite the colonies in 1776, until a new constitution was drafted in 1787. The federal government was slowly being organized under the guiding light of Washington, the members of the Continental government, and the finance department. The value of money continued to fluctuate, the government often ran out of funds, and foreign governments constantly propped up the new nation with loans.

Salomon's work involved high-level diplomatic finances. One of the most important diplomatic officials was Don Francisco de Rendon, who represented Charles III, king of Spain, as the unofficial ambassador of that country. While Rendon was in the United States, he turned to Haym Salomon to help pay his own expenses. Without Salomon's financial backing, the ambassador would have had to return to Spain. Rendon borrowed more than $10,000 from Salomon during his two-year stay in America. Salomon's support of such officials kept the lines of communication and the flow of funds open between the United States and Spain. In 1783, Don Francisco Rendon wrote:

This portrait of Charles III was painted by Francisco José de Goya y Lucientes. Here, Goya has depicted the king as a huntsman, equipped with a rifle and a dog.

> *Mr. Salomon has advanced the money for the service of his most Catholic Majesty, and I am indebted to his friendship, . . . for the support of my character as his most Catholic Majesty's agent here, with any degree of credit and reputation; and without it, I should not have been able to render that protection and assistance to his Majesty's subjects, that his Majesty enjoins and my duty requires.*

Salomon was instrumental in helping high-level French diplomats as well. When the Chevalier de La Luzerne became the ambassador of France, he appointed Salomon as the American banker for France. The amount of money that flowed back and forth between the United States and France, under Salomon's guidance, eventually totaled approximately $200,000, then an enormous sum. Salomon charged a commission for handling this large sum of money and then invested everything that he earned back into funds that supported the federal government.

Salomon's task of buying and selling bonds, bills, and foreign currency was a difficult one. There were some days when Salomon could not sell a single bond. This meant that whatever reserves of cash there were in the Bank of North America would have to cover immediate expenses.

The market set the value for bonds by demand: A high demand might raise the price of bonds, and a low demand might lower the price of bonds. For example, if ten people are willing to purchase a bond at a high price, a banker can be assured that he will find a buyer for the highly priced bond. If no one is willing to spend money on a highly priced bond then the bond, price must be lowered in the hope of attracting a buyer.

Money was often so tight that the bank had great difficulty covering government expenses. On May 8, 1782, for example, Robert Morris wrote:

> *This Morning I sent for Mr. Haym Salomon.*
> *He came and informs me that the interruption*
> *to our Commerce and the losses of the*
> *Merchants of this City has so dispirited the*

*Purchasers of Bills of Exchange that he cannot
make Sale at any Price.*

To calculate the value of currency, Robert Morris
and Haym Salomon relied on tables and charts, which
showed the actual gold and silver value behind the
money they dealt with on a daily basis. This value
changed from country to country. In June 1782, for
example, 1 English pound (.45 kg) of gold was cut into
approximately 44 guineas, and 1 pound (.45 kg) of silver

This is the type of scale a merchant or banker would use
to judge the value of coins. By weighing one coin against
another, a merchant could calculate the proper rate
of exchange of the two coins being weighed.

*Tuberculosis has plagued mankind since ancient times. Egyptian mummies from 2400 B.C. show signs of suffering from tuberculosis. In 1720, the British physician Benjamin Marten was the first to speculate that the disease was caused by a living organism that invaded the body. Furthermore, Doctor Marten also guessed that the disease could be passed from one person to another after prolonged contact. Modern doctors know that a patient who is given plenty of sunlight and fresh air is less likely to contract the disease. Haym Salomon was probably first exposed to the disease in the Old Sugar House, a dark, damp, and crowded British prison.*

was cut into 62 shillings. The pure metal was then mixed with different base metals. This process created what was known as an alloy. Because the amount of gold or silver and alloy in coins was different from country to country, the value of their coins differed as well. English money might contain more silver and gold than the money of Spain, France, Portugal, or Holland. This difference affected the real value of the money that it represented. For example, 1 pound of English silver coins in 1782 contained 5,328 grains of silver, whereas 1 pound of silver coins from France contained 5,220 grains of silver.

Even though the price of the money itself changed from day to day and from country to country, Morris and his advisers, including Salomon, decided what the money was worth by weighing the coins and then circulating them according to their market value. All the countries that traded with each other had to agree on a common exchange rate. This was necessary to achieve uniformity between the foreign currency and the American dollar.

While Salomon concentrated on keeping the federal government financially secure, he paid little attention to his own finances, collecting only a small percentage of interest on these government transactions. Salomon's cough, which began while he was in the British prisons, continued to grow worse. His doctors warned him that he could not continue to work at such a hectic pace. Salomon put his own financial and personal well being second to his duty to his country. Eventually, neglecting his health and his personal finances would cost him dearly.

# 10. Salomon's Fight for Religious Freedom

Salomon's private life was often pushed to the side because of his work for the new government. Although Salomon was rarely home to help raise his three children, his devotion to his family was unwavering. Salomon also never forgot the family that he had left behind in Poland. By 1782, Poland had been split up and divided between the three powerful counties at its borders, Russia, Prussia, and Austria. These countries had carved up Poland for themselves and had made life difficult for the Jews who lived there.

In January 1775, the Jews had been expelled from the great city of Warsaw, Poland, because they were not Christian. Salomon was concerned about this development when the news slowly made its way to him from Poland. During the war, Salomon was unable to send financial aid to his family because of the British blockade. By 1782, however, he sent 1,500 pounds to his parents and extended family. Salomon also enclosed a gold chain for his mother. Later Salomon paid the taxes that were required for his father to be allowed to remain in his town in Poland. Salomon's father no longer had to fear being expelled from his town. Salomon also acquired a burial ground for the Salomon family still in Poland and sent enough money to sponsor any young man in his family who wished to become a rabbi. Salomon added the condition, however, that anyone who wanted to do this must learn one of the "Christian languages," which were English, French, Spanish, German, and Italian. Salomon's life had been spared because he could speak seven European languages; this was the only reason the Hessian soldiers secured his release from the Provost Prison. If Salomon was going to support a young scholar,

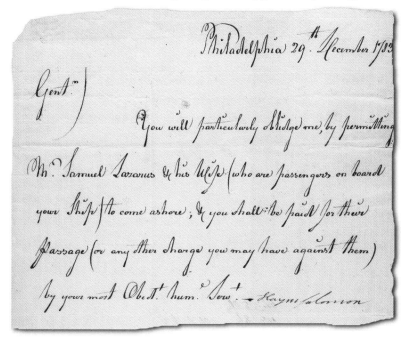

In this 1783 letter Haym Salomon promised to pay the shipboard passage for Samuel Lazarus and his wife. Their great-granddaughter Emma Lazarus would honor her ancestors and millions of other immigrants to America in her poem *The New Colossus*, which is inscribed on the pedestal of the Statue of Liberty in New York's harbor.

he wanted the young man to be armed with the linguistic gift of speaking in a language other than Yiddish. For Jews in Europe or the United States, being bilingual could make the difference between life and death.

Haym Salomon had remained a devout Jew in Philadelphia. He joined the Jewish congregation Mikveh Israel, which met in various homes during the American Revolution. After the war, the Jewish community began to raise funds to build a permanent synagogue. Salomon contributed some of the largest sums, paying one-quarter of the amount of the building costs. Haym Salomon also purchased a Torah for the new temple. A Torah is a religious scroll containing the first five books of the Bible.

In 1783, Haym Salomon, along with other members of the

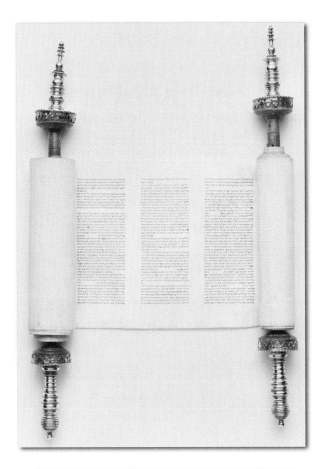

This Torah scroll was made in Nuremberg, Germany, between 1700–1751. Johann Conrad Weiss made the Torah's staves from silver and wood. The scroll is attached to the staves and then unrolled when it is read.

Jewish community, protested an earlier amendment to the state laws of Pennsylvania. This law denied full citizenship to Jews in Pennsylvania. The law demanded that any person holding public office must take a Christian oath of allegiance.

Such religious oaths, or religious tests as they were often called, had once been common in England. Members of the established Anglican Church had restricted public office to those who worshiped in the Anglican Church. In this way, the Church of England, as it was also called, sought to maintain control over a population that was increasingly open to Catholics and Protestants.

The Pennsylvanian law dismayed Salomon, as he and so many other Jews had sacrificed their lives and their fortunes for the new nation. Haym Salomon, along with Gershom Seixas, Barnard Gratz, Simon Nathan, Jonas Phillips, and Asher Myers, petitioned the Pennsylvania Council of Censors and demanded that the Christian test oath be removed as a requirement for public office. They stated:

> *Your memorialists [the petitioners] . . . with great submission . . . apprehend that a clause in the constitution, which disables them to be elected by their fellow citizens to represent them in assembly, is a stigma upon their nation and religion, and it is inconsonant with the second paragraph of the said bill of rights*

*. . . The Jews of Pennsylvania . . . have served some of them in the Continental army; some went out in the militia to fight the common enemy; all of them have cheerfully contributed to the support of the militia, and of the government of this State.*

Unfortunately, in 1783, the Pennsylvania Council did not omit the demand for a Christian oath before taking office. However, in 1790, Pennsylvania repealed the requirement for the oath. As a result, Pennsylvania was one of the first states to provide broad religious freedom, allowing people of all faiths to hold public office. The original protest led by Salomon and others from the Congregation Mikveh Israel set the stage for later reform.

The right to freedom of religion was formally established in the United States with the First Amendment of the Bill of Rights in 1791. These amendments to the U.S. Constitution were championed by James Madison, a Virginian delegate to the Constitutional Convention, who made certain that a citizen's right to freedom of religion, speech, freedom of the press, peaceful assembly, and the right to petition were written into law.

In 1784, doctor's diagnosed Salomon's terrible cough as consumption. Today we call this disease tuberculosis. Tuberculosis is a respiratory illness that is caused by bacteria attacking the lungs, which may eventually lead to death. Salomon was hoping to establish a second mercantile and brokerage business in New York City and had entered into a partnership with Jacob Mordecai. Mordecai and Salomon had found an office on Wall Street, but Salomon's health was failing. Before Haym Salomon died, he wrote a letter to his clerk, acknowledging his desire to retire from his business. Salomon wrote, "The public securities I have, being considerable,

This bill of sale records the sale of Salomon's wholesale goods at auction to store owners on March 5, 1784. Among the goods sold were pocketbooks, buttons, warming pans, and shoes. Salomon's profit from the auction was calculated after the auction house fees and advertising fees were paid.

(some $350,000,) I wish to make inquiry what could be done with them. . . ."

Salomon hoped to get full value for his investments. Although he was dying, he had provided well for his family with $350,000 credit in government securities. Haym Salomon died on January 6, 1785. Salomon was a man who had braved the icy North

Established in 1738, Mikveh Israel Cemetery is the oldest Jewish cemetery in Philadelphia. Salomon was laid to rest in this cemetery although his gravestone is unmarked. The memorial, left, was placed in 1976. The tablet, right, was erected by Haym Salomon's great-grandson William Salomon in 1917, and declares Salomon a patriot.

Country, had fought alongside the founding fathers to raise funds for the American Revolution, and had given both moral and financial support to his Jewish community. He was forty-five years old. In the Philadelphia paper the *Pennsylvania Packet* a notice announced Salomon's death:

> *January 11, 1785*
>
> *Thursday last, expired, after a lingering illness, Mr. Haym Salomons, an eminent broker of this city; he was a native of Poland, and of the*

*Hebrew nation. He was remarkable for his skill and integrity in his profession, and for his generous and human deportment. His remains were on Friday last deposited in the burial ground of the synagogue, in this city.*

Salomon's wife, Rachel, was a widow at the age of twenty-three. She was left with three young children and an infant, named Haym, to raise on her own. Rachel was not certain how to go about collecting the money that was owed to the family, the $350,000 that Salomon had invested in government securities. The state of Pennsylvania asked Rachel for the certificates and securities that Salomon had purchased. Although Rachel did this, she never received payment for them. Later, when the family pursued the matter, they were told that the certificates had been "lost."

After his death, Salomon's creditors collected what was owed to them, $45,292. As the family only possessed $44,732, Rachel was still in debt for the remaining $560 that was owed. Salomon was not the only patriot to lose his entire life savings to the cause. Robert Morris also died a penniless man. Many of the founding fathers gave everything they possessed in order to establish the United States of America.

Rachel later married David Heilbron in 1786. Her daughter Sarah married Joseph Andrews in 1794, and Deborah married Simon Myers Cohen in 1801. Her oldest son, Ezekiel, became the head of the United States Bank in New Orleans, and her youngest son, Haym M., became a merchant.

Haym Salomon's descendants applied to Congress in 1846 and again in 1869 to be compensated for the monies that they felt were owed to them. Unfortunately, they never collected any money from the government securities that Salomon himself had made secure through his own financial investments.

The name of Haym Salomon, however, has never been forgotten. Two statues were erected in his honor, one in Los Angeles, California, in Mac Arthur Park and another in Chicago, Illinois, where Haym Salomon and Robert Morris stand on either side of George Washington. When President Franklin D. Roosevelt heard of the intended monument in Chicago, he wrote on August 24, 1936:

> *I am indeed gratified to learn that belated recognition is to be made of the invaluable services rendered to the cause of the American Revolution by Haym Salomon. History was for a long time strangely silent concerning the unselfish and munificent financial support accorded the struggling colonies by this Philadelphia banker.*

Later in honor of the dedication of the statue in Chicago, President Franklin D. Roosevelt wrote on November 13, 1941:

The George Washington, Robert Morris, and Haym Salomon
Memorial in Chicago, Illinois, was designed by the artist
Lorado Zadoc Taft. The alderman Barnet Hodes created the
Patriotic Foundation to raise the money needed to build this
monument. This photograph was taken at the unveiling in 1941.

*The strength of the American cause in the War of the Revolution lay in the fact that in every critical phase of the contest the right leaders were raised up to perform whatever task needed to be done. . . . Two financiers on whom Washington leaned heavily in the darkest hours of the Revolution were Haym Salomon and Robert Morris. Their genius in finance and fiscal affairs and unselfish devotion to the cause of liberty made their support of the utmost importance when the struggling colonies were fighting against such heavy odds.*

*It is, therefore, especially appropriate that this great triumvirate of patriots—George Washington, Robert Morris, and Haym Salomon—should be commemorated together in Chicago. The memorial which you are about to dedicate will stand as an inspiration to generations yet unborn to place love of country above every selfish end.*

In 1975, a stamp was commissioned by the U.S. Post Office to recognize Haym Salomon as a contributor to the American Revolution and to the founding of this great nation.

In the struggle for the rights to life, liberty, and the pursuit of happiness, as Thomas Jefferson so eloquently wrote in the Declaration of Independence, Haym Salomon gave of himself completely. He sacrificed his

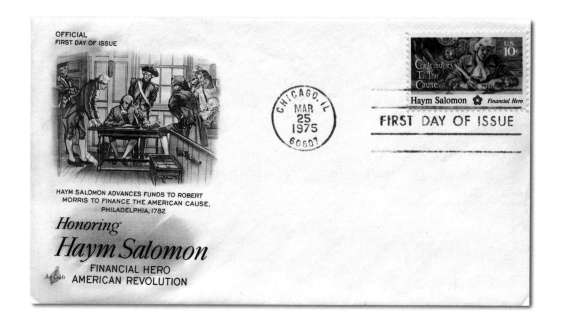

A stamp honoring Haym Salomon, called Financial Hero,
was issued by the U.S. Post Office in 1975 as part of
a series honoring contributors to the cause.

time, his money, and ultimately his life to establish a
great country. Haym Salomon helped to finance the
American Revolution and to put the country on sound
financial ground after it was established. Salomon's
genius in financial affairs helped the leaders of the
American Revolution to win the war and to create a
strong United States of America.

# Timeline

| | |
|---|---|
| **1740** | Haym Salomon is born in Lissa, Poland. |
| **1764** | Salomon leaves his family because of the heavy taxes established for Jews. |
| | Salomon might have arrived in New York City. |
| **1770** | The Liberty Boys gather around the liberty pole in New York City. When British soldiers tear down the pole, the Liberty Boys rebuild it. |
| **1775** | Haym Salomon is a busy merchant in New York City when the Battle of Lexington and Concord is fought on April 19. |
| **1776** | Salomon asks Leonard Gansevoort to recommend him to General Schuyler. Gansevoort agrees. |
| | Haym Salomon travels to Fort Ticonderoga as a sutler. |
| | Salomon is arrested and sent to the Provost Prison after a fire in New York City on September 20. |
| **1777** | Haym Salomon and Rachel Franks are married in New York City on July 6. |
| | Salomon's merchant shop is so successful that he moves his establishment nearer to New York City's business district. |
| **1778** | A patriot is suspected of setting New York City on fire, and Salomon flees to Philadelphia on August 5. |
| | Salomon writes to the Continental Congress on August 25 and offers his services to the government. |

| | |
|---|---|
| **1779** | Salomon becomes a broker for the French consulate and to the paymaster-general. |
| **1781** | On February 20, Robert Morris becomes the superintendent of finance. |
| | Salomon represents Morris as a broker on June 8. |
| | Salomon raises $20,000 to finance Washington's march to Yorktown. |
| | Salomon becomes a leader of his Philadelphia congregation Mikveh Israel. |
| **1782** | On January 7, the Bank of North America opens. Haym Salomon is one of the first investors in this bank. |
| | On July 12, Salomon becomes the official broker to the office of finance. |
| **1783** | The Treaty of Paris ends the American Revolution on September 3. |
| | Salomon joins a fight for religious freedom in Pennsylvania. Salomon and other members of the Jewish community petition the Pennsylvania government to allow Jewish citizens to hold public office. |
| **1784** | Salomon attempts to establish a broker mercantile business in New York City. |
| | Salomon's cough is diagnosed as consumption, a disease that is later known as tuberculosis. |
| **1785** | Haym Salomon dies on January 6. |
| **1941** | A monument is erected in Chicago, Illinois, which honors Haym Salomon, Robert Morris, and George Washington. This monument acknowledges the contribution these patriots made to the American Revolution. |

# Glossary

**barricades** (BAR-uh-kaydz) Things that are fortified with an obstacle that hinders the approach of an enemy.

**bartering** (BAR-tur-ing) Trading something to obtain something else.

**bateaux** (ba-TOH) A flat-bottomed boat that usually has flared sides.

**bigotry** (BIG-ah-tree) An action taken against someone because of his or her race or religion.

**bills of exchange** (BILZ UV iks-CHAYNJ) Signed documents that state the amount of money to be loaned and the date upon which it must be repaid.

**blockades** (blah-KAYDZ) Ships that block passage to ports by ships of another country.

**broker** (BROH-kur) A middleman who helps people buy and sell contracts.

**chandler** (CHAND-ler) A person who supplies a ship with goods for a voyage.

**commodities** (kuh-MAH-duh-teez) Something that is bought or sold.

**commemorative** (kuh-MEM-ruh-tiv) Something that is created to honor a person, a place, or an event.

**creditors** (KREH-dih-turz) People to whom money or goods are owed. People who make loans.

**currency** (KUR-en-see) Money.

**distiller** (dih-STIH-ler) A person who makes alcoholic beverages through a process called distillation.

**entrenched** (in-TRENCHD) To have dug or occupied a trench for defensive purposes.

**exported** (ek-SPORT-ed ) Sold and transported a product to another country.

**fluency** (FLOO-en-see) The state of being able to do something with ease, such as speak another language.

**gondolas** (GAHN-duh-luz) Small boats with flat bottoms.

**government securities** (GUH-vurn-mint sih-KYUR-ih-teez) Government certificates or bonds that are used as currency.

**Hessians** (HEH-shenz) German soldiers who were paid to fight for the British during the American Revolution.

**immigrant** (IH-muh-grint) Someone who moves to a new country from another country.

**Inquisition** (in-kwuh-ZIH-shun) A tribunal set up to investigate heresy, or opinions that differed from accepted church beliefs.

**integrity** (in-TEH-grih-tee) Honesty; the support of ideas in which you believe.

**interpreter** (in TER-prih-ter) Someone who helps people who speak different languages talk to each other.

**invaluable** (in-VAL-yuh-bul) So valuable that the value cannot be estimated.

**linguistic** (ling-GWIS-tik) Relating to language, or the study of differences in language.

**militia** (muh-LIH-shuh) A group of volunteer or citizen soldiers who are organized to assemble in emergencies.

**probation** (proh-BAY-shun) Being under the supervision of a court-appointed officer.

**redeemed** (ree-DEEMD) To have bought something back, or to have exchanged an item for something that is better.

**sanction** (SANK-shun) To give formal approval or consent to something.

**specie** (SPEE-shee) Coin that is used to buy and sell goods as opposed to paper money.

**strategized** (STRA-tuh-jized) To have used the science of planning and directing large military movements.

**Tory** (TOR-ee) A loyalist, or a colonist in support of British rule.

# Additional Resources

If you would like to learn more about Haym Salomon, check out the following books and Web sites:

## Books

Brilliant, Richard. *Facing the New World: Jewish Portraits in Colonial and Federal America*. New York: Prestel, 1997.

Knight, Vick, Jr. *Send for Haym Salomon!* Alhambra, CA: Borden Publishing Company, 1976.

## Web Sites

Due to the changing nature of Internet links, PowerPlus Books has developed an online list of Web sites related to the subject of this book. This site is updated regularly. Please use this link to access the list: www.powerkidslinks.com/lalt/hsalomon/

# Bibliography

Bellico, Russell P. *Chronicles of Lake Champlain: Journeys in War and Peace*. Fleischmanns, NY: Purple Mountain Press, 1999.

"Bridewell Prison." <www.scripophily.net/dewclinsigch.html>.

Commager, Henry Steele and Richard B. Morris, eds. *The Spirit of 'Seventy-Six: The Story of the American Revolution as Told by Participants*. New York: Da Capo Press, 1995.

Durkee. "The Committee on Revolutionary Claims, to whom was referred the memorial of Haym M. Salomon, for indemnity for advances of money made by his father during the revolutionary war, have had the same under consideration, and respectfully report." Washington D.C.: The Senate of the United States, March 9, 1880.

Gansevoort, Leonard. Letter from Leonard Gansevoort to Philip Schuyler, June 12, 1776 (concerning Haym Salomon), held in the Philip Schuyler Papers, Manuscripts & Archives Division, The New York Public Library, Astor, Lenox and Tilden Foundations.

"Haym Salomon" United States Jewry, 1776–1985. Detroit: Wayne State UP, 1989.

Kammen, Michael G. *Colonial New York: A History*. New York: Scribner Publishing Company, 1975.

Knight, Vick, Jr. *Send for Haym Salomon!* Alhambra, CA: Borden Publishing Company, 1976.

"Liberty Bell Timeline." Independence Hall Association. <www.ushistory.org>.

Marcus, Jacob Rader. *Early American Jewry*. Philadelphia: Jewish Publication Society of America, 1951–1953.

Martin, James Kirby. *Benedict Arnold, Revolutionary Hero: An American Warrior Reconsidered*. New York: New York University Press, 1997.

Palmer, Peter S. *History of Lake Champlain From its First Exploration by the French in 1609 to the Close of the Year 1814.* Fleischmanns, NY: Purple Mountain Press, 1992.

*Revolutionary Soldier, The, 1775–1783.* Old Saybrook, CT: The Globe Pequot Press, 1993.

Rezneck, Samuel. *Unrecognized Patriots: The Jews in the American Revolution.* Westport, CT: Greenwood Press, 1975.

Roosevelt, Franklin Delano. "Letter to Mr. Hodes: Co-Chairman of the Patriotic Foundation of Chicago." Washington, D.C.: The White House, August 24, 1936.

Salomon, Haym. "August 25, 1778 Memorial Haym Salomon." Curtesy of The Jacob Rader Marcus Center of The American Jewish Archives, Hebrew Union College, Cincinnati, OH.

Schappes, Morris U. "Excerpts From Robert Morris' 'Diaries in the Office of Finance, 1781–1784,' Referring to Haym Salomon and Other Jews." *American Jewish Historical Quarterly.* LXVII (1977):9-49.

Schouler, James. *Americans of 1776: Daily Life in Revolutionary America.* Gansevoort, NY: Corner House Historical Publications, 1999.

Schwartz, Laurens R. *Jews and the American Revolution: Haym Salomon and Others.* Jefferson, NC: McFarland, 1987.

Tallmadge. "The Committee on Revolutionary Claims, to whom was referred the memorial of Haym M. Salomon, legal representative of Haym Salomon, deceased, report." Washington D.C.: House of Representative, April 26, 1848.

Van Tyne, Claude Halstead, Ph.D. *Loyalists in the American Revolution.* Gansevoort, NY: Corner House Historical Publications, 1999.

Wilbur, C. Keith. *Pirates & Patriots of the Revolution.* Old Saybrook, CT: The Globe Pequot Press, 1993.

# Index

# About the Author

Jane Frances Amler is the internationally recognized author of *Christopher Columbus's Jewish Roots*, a main selection of the Jewish Book Club. She also writes for the Scribner Encyclopedia of American Lives. She holds a Ph.D. in creative writing/English literature and teaches writing at Manhattan College in New York City. She lives in New York with her husband and two sons.

# Primary Sources

**Cover**. *Haym Salomon*, oil painting, ca. 1800s, Haym Salomon Home for the Aged, Brooklyn, NY., Bill of credit issued by the Bank of North America on August 6, 1789, Department of Special Collections at the University Libraries of Notre Dame. **Page 4**. See cover. **Page 7**. Map of Poland, 1773, Thomas Kitchin, Map Division, The New York Public Library, Astor, Lenox and Tilden Foundations. **Page 8**. *Displaying the Torah in the Portuguese Synagogue*, engraving and etching, ca. 1781, drawn by J. Buys, engraved and etched by C. Philips Jacobszoon, Jewish Theological Seminary of America. **Page 9**. *Stanislaw August Poniatowski II*, oil painting, 1802, Élizabeth Vigée-Lebrun, Giraudon/Bridgeman Art Library. **Page 10**. Proof sheet of official tax stamps, 1765, The British Library. **Page 12**. *Liberty Pole*, Pen and ink drawing, 1770, P. E. Du Simitière, The Library Company of Philadelphia. **Page 14**. Sons of Liberty Broadside, 1775, printed by John Holt, Library of Congress, Rare Book and Special Collections Division. **Page 19**. *The Battle of Lexington Green*, engraving, 1775, Amos Doolittle, Print Collection, Miriam and Ira D. Wallach Division of Arts, Prints, and Photographs, The New York Public Library, Astor, Lenox, and Tilden Foundations. **Page 21**. Philip Schuyler, oil painting, 1881, Jacob Lazarus, created from an earlier work by John Trumbull, Schuyler Mansion State Historic Site New York State Office of Parks, Recreation and Historic Preservation. **Page 22**. *The Death of General Montgomery in the Attack on Quebec, December 31, 1775*, oil painting, 1786, John Trumbull, Francis G. Mayer/CORBIS. **Page 24**. *Provisions in sight!*, engraving, 1903, drawn by Denman Fink, engraved by F. H. Wellington, Library of Congress Prints and Photographs Division. **Page 25**. Plan of Carillon ou [sic] Ticonderoga, detail from a map of Fort Carillon, later named Fort Ticonderoga, pen-and-ink, watercolors, and wash, 1777, Michel Capitaine du Chesnoy, Library of Congress Geography and Map Division. **Page 28**. Canteen, wood and iron, ca. 1750–1870, The George C. Neumann Collection, Valley Forge National Historical Park. **Page 30**. *Battle of Valcour Island, A view of the New England Arm'd vessels in Valcour Bay on Lake C[hamplain], 11 October 1776*, ca. 1776, watercolor, C. Randle, Archives of Canada. **Page 33**. *Der Einzug der Koniglichen Volcker in Neu Yorck L'Entré triumphale de troupes royales a Nouvelle Yorck, 1776* (British soldiers occupying New York, 1776), engraving, etching, 1776, Franz Xaver Habermann, Library of Congress Prints and Photographs. **Page 34–35**. *Representation Du Feu Terrible A Nouvelle Yorck* (Representation of the Terrible Fire in New York), engraving, ca. 1780, Franz Xaver Habermann, Anne S. K. Brown Military Collection, Brown University Library. **Page 39**. *John Ulrich Zeth, a Hessian Soldier*, watercolor, ca. 1777, Friedrich Konstantin von Germann, Print Collection, Miriam and Ira D. Wallach Division of Art, Prints, and Photographs, New York Public Library, Astor, Lenox, and Tilden Foundations. **Page 44**. Ketubah of Haym Salomon and Rachel Franks, ink on paper, 1777, American Jewish Historical Society. **Page 47**. Liberty Bell, 1753, first cast by the White Chapel Bell Foundry of London in 1752, later recast, twice, in Philadelphia by John Pass and John Stow in 1753, Leif Skoogfors/CORBIS. **Page 48**. *William Howe*, mezzotint, 1777, C. Corbutt, Anne S. K. Brown Military Collection, Brown University Library. **Page 49**. *Washington Sees the Bloody Footprints in the Snow*, 1907, John Ward Dunsmore, Library of Congress Prints and Photographs Division. **Page 51**. *The New-York Gazette, and the weekly Mercury*, newspaper clipping from September 1, 1777, Rare Books & Manuscripts Collection, New York Public Library Astor, Lenox, and Tilden Foundations. **Page 55**. *View of Philadelphia, 1776*, pen and ink and wash, Archibald Robertson, Spencer Collection, the New York Public Library, Astor Lenox, and Tilden Foundations. **Page 58**. Haym Salomon's letter to Congress from August 25, 1778, the American Jewish Archives. **Page 62**. Bill of exchange from December 14, 1780, American Jewish Historical Society. **Page 65**. Robert Morris, oil painting, ca. 1782, C. W. Peale, Independence National Historical Park. **Page 66**. French bill of exchange from June 16, 1784, American Jewish Historical Society. **Page 69**. *George Washington*, oil painting, ca. 1785, Robert Edge Pime, Independence National Historical Park, **Page 71**. *(top)* Study for *The Surrender of Lord Cornwallis*, oil sketch, 1787, John Trumbull, Detroit Institute of the Arts; *(bottom)* *The Surrender of Lord Cornwallis*, oil painting, 1817, John Trumbull, Architect of the Capital. **Page 74**. See cover. **Page 79**. *Signing of the Treaty of Paris, 1782*, oil painting, 1783, Benjamin West, Winterthur Museum. **Page 81**. *James Madison*, pastel, ca. 1796, James Sharples, Independence National Historical Park. **Page 83**. *Charles III*, Francisco de Goya y Lucientes, Scala/Art Resource, N.Y. **Page 89**. Letter from Haym Salomon written on December 29, 1783, offering to pay the transatlantic fare for the grandparents of Emma Lazarus, Jewish Theological Seminary. **Page 90**. Torah scroll and staves from Nurmeberg, scroll is ink on vellum, staves are wood and silver, ca. 1700–1751, staves and fittings by Johann Conrad Weiss, The Jewish Museum, NY/Art Resource, N.Y. **Page 93**. Bill of sale from March 5, 1784, goods sold at auction by Haym Salomon, American Jewish Historical Society.

# Credits

## Photo Credits

Cover (portrait), p. 4 courtesy of Haym Salomon Home for the Aged, Brooklyn, NY Gift of Mrs. H. Altshiler; Cover (background), p. 74 Reproduced from the original held by the Department of Special Collections at the University Libraries of Notre Dame; Cover (scale), pp. 17, 85 Colonial Williamsburg Foundation; p. 7 courtesy of Map Division, The New York Public Library, Astor, Lenox, and Tilden Foundations; pp. 8, 89 Jewish Theological Seminary of America; p. 9 Giraudon/Bridgeman Art Library; p. 11 The British Library; p. 12 The Library Company of Philadelphia; p. 14 Library of Congress, Rare Book and Special Collections Division; pp. 19, 39 Print Collection, Miriam and Ira D. Wallach Division of Arts, Prints, and Photographs, The New York Public Library, Astor, Lenox, and Tilden Foundations; p. 21 courtesy, Schuyler Mansion State Historic Site New york State Office of Parks, Recreation and Historic Preservation; p. 22 © Francis G. Mayer/CORBIS; pp. 24, 33, 49 Library of Congress Prints and Photographs; p. 25 Library of Congress Geography and Map Division; p. 28 The George C. Neumann Collection, Valley Forge National Historical Park, VAFO 1054; p. 30 U.S. Navy Historical Center; pp. 34–35, 48 Anne S.K. Brown Military Collection, Brown University Library; p. 37 Culver Pictures; pp. 43, 44, 62, 66, 93 American Jewish Historical Society; p. 45 The New-York Historical Society; p. 47 © Leif Skoogfors/CORBIS; p. 51 courtesy of the Rare Books & Manuscripts Collection, New York Public Library, Astor, Lenox, and Tilden Foundations; p. 55 Spencer Collection, the New York Public Library, Astor, Lenox, and Tilden Foundations; p. 58 American Jewish Archives; p. 59 Mikveh Israel; pp. 65, 69, 81 Independence National Historical Park; p. 71 (top) Detroit Institute of the Arts; p. 72 (bottom) Architect of the Capitol; p. 79 courtesy, Winterthur Museum, gift of Henry F. du Pont; p. 83 Scala/Art Resource, NY; p. 90 The Jewish Museum, NY/Art Resource, NY; p. 94 Maura B. McConnell; p. 97 Chicago Historical Society; p. 99 Collection of Roger Rosen.

## Project Editor
Daryl Heller

## Series Design
Laura Murawski

## Layout Design
Corinne L. Jacob

## Photo Researcher
Jeffrey Wendt